Under The Pier

Salena Godden

Nasty Little Press

Published by Nasty Little Press in February 2011.

Nasty Little Press
35 St Johns Road
Bungay
Suffolk

nastylittlepress.org

Printed and bound by Print-X
7 Edgefield Close
Whitchurch
Bristol

ISBN: 978-0-9563767-4-9

A CIP record of this book is available
from the British Library.

Nasty Little Press gratefully ackowledges the support of
Arts Council England.

The Little Dog Laughed

I was walking beside you in Hastings
with your funny sausage dog
pulling us down London Road
past the Queen Victoria and along the seafront

and when we got to the White Rock Theatre
we went up to the balcony for tea but
the pier was still there, oh dear, I cried
for then I knew I was in a dream

the pier was still there, and you,
you were still with us.

These poems are dedicated to my family.
In memory of my Grandpa, George and my Nanny, Muriel.

Acknowledgements

Early drafts of some of these poems were published in Rising Magazine. Acknowlegement and thanks to Tim Wells for all his support over the years, keep fighting the good fight!"

Contents

There Was Tenderness

Do you remember?
You dandled me on your knee
you blew raspberries on my naked flesh
put your mouth to my skin
blew hard with trumpet lips
and wet my navel.

I don't remember minding
in fact I encouraged this behaviour
I would have been chuckling
besides if it had troubled me
I doubt I would have been able to fight you off
considering.

Maybe this will jog your memory
you cannot forget this:
it is highly likely I took a piss
whilst sitting in your lap
I sported material
fastened with a safety pin
around my nether regions
which leaked.

I would have dribbled too, no doubt,
I was prone to dribbling

you see, I hadn't bothered to grow teeth
yet. I might have had one tooth
ripping forth at the front
it would have caused me great pains
you let me chew gummily on your finger.

I was probably out of it on Calpol
and I made very little sense.
I gurgled and made *coo-coo* sounds.
Admittedly my language was limited
but I may have said *Dada*
thrown it in casually
to keep my end up
and contribute to proceedings.

Oh, and I was bald, well, almost
except for some gold wisps
of feathery white curls
at the crown of my head.
You would have pressed your lips
against them and inhaled
slowly and surely
steadily breathing me in
capturing the smell of me.

You may not recognise me
with my clothes on?
I was chubbier then
buddha-shaped

pot-bellied
soft and pale and small
compelled
to suck my own toes.
It was easier then, you see,
they were closer to my mouth
than they are now.

I was the one.
It was me that couldn't find my own mouth
with a spoon of mashed bananas
and I sicked up milk
in fat and gentle burps.
Now do you remember?
It is highly likely this produced a stain
a mark that spoiled the shoulder of your jacket
which was either velvet or corduroy or suede
a peacock green, ink blue
red wine, burgundy…
I suddenly don't remember which
but it would have been a bitch
to wipe off.

I wonder if any of this rings a bell?
I know I would have been with a woman
she went everywhere with me back then
she watched me incessantly
she'd chase me if I tried to crawl away
she stopped me sticking my fingers in plug sockets

and snatched me up into her bosom
when I tried to drink shampoo or eat the cat's food.

She even took it upon herself
to harness me to her chest
or wheel me around the streets
in all weathers
in a sort of moveable bed.
I was all wrapped up in a pink blanket
I never had to walk anywhere then
which was a sweet gig
because I could only just stand up
on my own two feet.

The woman,
yes, you must remember her?
She was a fit sort
highly accommodating
glittery dark eyes and a bright smile
most of all she had very lovely long smooth legs
and she kept getting her breasts out
to put her tit in my mouth
which was something that was required.
She was up for it though
and she did it all the time
even in the middle of the night
even in public.

She cleaned up all my mess
factored in my every need
and celebrated the smallest things,
the faces I pulled learning to smile,
my preoccupation with eating mud.
What a sport and
what a super nice lady
she gave me such loving.
She is still knocking around,
says she loves me.
One of these days
I really must find some way to thank her
properly.

And she sang to me
in fact you both did
you sang duets
merrily merrily merrily merrily
life is but a dream
you both watched me fall asleep
as though you had nothing better to do
of an evening.

Do you remember?
you dandled me on your knee.
I remember
I have to remember that

I mean
I make a point of making sure
to never forget these things.
It comes sometimes
in the blink of an eye
on the tip of my tongue
triggered by a sensation of warmth
or a certain trick in the light,
a flicker of flame in a sunset
at the end of the dying day,
this yellowing snapshot
a faint shape of you
your sideburns against my cheek,
my own chubby hand grabbing your chest hairs
sprouting out above the neck of your vest.
You wore a crucifix or was it
a St Christopher on a chain?

Sometimes in the silence between heart beats
I can call upon a sound,
a heat of you
being there
the woman
and the man
laughing
high above my head
there was tenderness

and strain
the woman crying
tears streaking her face
banging my back
agitated
swinging me from hip to hip
as you sulk and skit
guilty and shadowy
as smoke.

Sour booze
morning breath
scratched burnt toast
a cold cup of tea
milk forming a skin
the boat setting sail.
You must leave
we knew this
we know this now.
But not until
you were going
going
gone.

Patti Smith

In a Greek bar, drinking ouzo
in Saint Michel
with a pencilled moustache like Dali
I see a familiar figure
in a big coat
woolly hat and spectacles
peering in the window

Oi, Patti!
I holler, chasing her
up the street.
PATTI!
I yell
Excuse me, are you?

She takes off her glasses
and shakes my hand
I say
It would be a great honour
for you to join us for a drink.

So softly
she replies
Oh man, I can't
I gotta work
back in my hotel room…

Her voice is so soft and gentle it
throws me.

Star-struck
I search my pockets for a gift
some present
to give her.

I find my black eye pencil
and blurt
Then can I give you a moustache
like mine?

She looks at my face
and says:
I was kinda
born with one

a deathly silence.
I say *oh*
oh yes
yes oh
um

we shake hands
and then she is gone
lost in the crowds
of Saint Michel.

Under The Pier

Under the pier
I'd meet you here
on Saturday lunchtimes
in technicolours and rainbows.

There were four of us that day
walking along Bottle Alley
I'd touch shards of saffron-coloured glass
pressed into the bleached concrete
and wonder what came in yellow bottles.

Ceri balanced along the ledge
like a gymnast on a beam
her wild gold hair trapped
in the corners of her mouth.

Claire wore thick mascara
in turquoise and royal blue
her eyelashes were insects
bluebottles and beetles legs.

Becky was tall and gangly
we talked about suicide.
We believed 1987
was gonna be just like 1967

as we swigged from the Thunderbirds Red
fifty pence more expensive
than the blue
but we were all sick of scrumpy.

The four of us sheltered there from
the rain and the boys and our parents.
It was our secret place
that nook and ledge

with our backs against the sea wall
our voices drowned out
by the crashing of waves
a wash of froth and brine
an echo of footsteps
across the soft rotting wood
of the boardwalk above us.

There were gaps between the planks
prisms of watery light
brown broken pipes emptied
in slurps of sewage.

Lightning flashed
between the rusty barnacled legs
of the dear old lady pier
and the magic mushrooms
made the sea all blood and ink.

We shared ten B&H
bubble-gum lip gloss
smeared and slipped off the tip
and the lip of the bottle
and we sang *Purple Rain*
memorised the words like a prayer.

With a tiny crumb of hash
we huddled around the light
we cupped our hands
to make the spliff, right,
we were grounded
because we had lovebites
we were nearly fifteen
and we had catfights.

We swore to be best friends forever
that our children would play together
one for all and all for one
forever and ever…

And as the storm died
the rain stopped and
God was a solitary shaft of sunlight
hitting the sea with a silver path to the horizon,

Under the pier
I'll meet you
here.

Then Men Burst In

No – I mean yes.
Come in.
We've been expecting you, in a weird way
it was inevitable you'd come
one day.

Come on through – careful!
Glass! Don't cut yourself –
I do wish you'd come in the front door though.

Sometimes it makes me jump
when people shout *Mrs Osborne!*
It's taking a while to get used to my new name.
Actually
we were just thinking about having a gin and tonic
would you care for one?

Oh ping! That'll be the oven
I'll be with you in a jiffy
would you like some shortbread?
I've been baking Mr Osborne's favourite.
Excuse the mess
we've been having a sort out
wedding photos and things
the pair of us are such hoarders.

Ah yes! Great cover, isn't it?
Be careful because that's a first edition
and our only copy.

Oh please don't...
that's John and I
when we read together on the Bowery
New York was brilliant.
We stayed at the Chelsea Hotel.

No! Not that one above the piano!
Do you mind? Please put it down!
That one is the most precious of all.
That's us on our wedding day
We got married at sea
sailing around the coast of Sicily.

We had a feast fit for Bacchus
french champagne, pina coladas
flaming sambucas.
It took us a while to get our sea legs
rocking to and fro on deck
sprayed with ocean mist
the taste of salt on our skin.

There were majestic sun rises in magenta
and magnificent sunsets
magently
that was our word, John and I,

we call last summer
magentle.

We cruised in our sailboat
around the Aeolian islands
Soaking in the mythology.
see those rocks there? That's where
they say Medusa and the sirens reigned and
look, this one is Aurora racing her chariots
across the horizon.

At dawn we laid on the bow
listening to the soft green lapping water
watching the big sky and holding hands.

For the wedding breakfast we ordered quince
and John and I laughed because
we didn't even know if we liked it.
We married at midnight
under the full moon
Sirius shone brightly above.
All the speeches were nice and short
haikus mostly.

Look how brown and tanned we all are there
jet ski-ing and scuba diving
hiking Stromboli
and in the distance you can just about make out Mount Etna
Oh, that's John surfing

you pulled off such a wicked aerial barrel roll that day
didn't you dear?

Oh please
don't please
don't take my wedding ring.
it was given to us by a bearded gypsy who looked like a pig
and do you know?
The priest even looked like a turkey.
Yes, everyone says that,
everyone says we are the owl and the pussycat
oh and he is my owl
look at him with his kind eyes
looking up at you now.
The John and the Lena went to sea in a beautiful pea green boat…
the happiest day of my life.

Listen, we know why you are here
we knew perfectly well you'd come one day
but the truth is we don't have any real valuables
we are just newlywed poets
I don't know why John led you on so.

We do know some famous writers
some of our friends are quite successful
you can have their signed books if you like
they might be worth something
one day.

Sorry, what did you say?
You know, you really are going to have to take that thing off.
I simply cannot hear you
mumbling
through that balaclava.

By The Flower Stall In Kings Cross I Sat Down And Wept
(after Elizabeth Smart)

Meet me at two thirty by the flower stall in Kings Cross.
I will take you to Edinburgh, where the last page is framed.

We were drunk with jasmine
and orange blossom
in Valencia,
where the swallows flew
into the window glass.

Where are you?
Which hospital ward
do you lie in
refusing to see me?

I didn't mean
that we'd never speak
ever again.

You have cancer.
It's serious.
They say it's for the best
they keep your whereabouts a secret
they tell me that I should
just leave it.

Being taught a lesson
but I already couldn't
unlearn you.

I forget the crimes
where we went wrong
the messes we made.
I find it impossible
to measure darkness
just absence of light.

You started it,
you, leaning over the bar.
Get your passport, you said
I'm taking you for dinner.
I asked: *And what will you drink?*
Cider and you, you smiled
and you, in Spain.

We made sad love,
the roof leaking rain
into buckets around the bed.
In our bubble it would be alright,
but then I woke up crying.

Now a gold June sunrise
forbids me to sleep
swallows swoop by
but they don't fly into my window pane,

smack
into reflections.

I pound and punish these keys
in some vain attempt to reach you
but it's a letter
I'll never post.

By the flower stall in Kings Cross
I sat down and wept.
Then I went to Edinburgh
where the last page is framed
this book I read
remembering you,
love,
for there was a time
when you could not pass
anywhere near me
without every drop of my blood
springing to attention.

A slammed door
the last word
and goodbye.

We were stubborn.
I'm sorry
and afraid to face you sick
and in pain

to see you how I left you
but worse.

If I could I'd read you
these lost last lines –
until the rocks melt
and the sea runs dry
my rose,
my bloody
bloodied rose.

The Boy in the Bay in May

I gazed into the water
the green and blue of his eyes
and lost my thread
                in the middle
of what I was trying to say.

He smiled
and we both stopped speaking

grinning at things left unsaid
lost mid-sentence.

It took my breath away
when he took me firmly around the waist
and kissed me hard
against the wall of a
narrow cobbled alleyway.

At closing time
we swigged whiskey
under Gemini stars
and beneath a yellowy moon
we snogged in a churchyard.

And much later
when I told him
don't do that
or you will make me
fall in love with you

he did it more
and more and more
as though he had
a capacity for love
and as though he wanted me
to fall in love with him

and for a moment
I fell in love
with the boy
that swam
in the bay
for the day
like May
flies.

When They Took Her Away

When they took her away
she wasn't kicking or screaming.
It was as though
she saw it coming
like she'd been buying time.
I wanted her to shake her fist
tell us she'd show us one day
I thought she'd put up a fight
instead,

when they took her away –
they didn't take her away exactly,
but they led her away –
I saw her lips in a silent whistle
she was exhaling with one breath
she was blowing out a candle
at the end of the night.

As she got into the back seat
they protected her head
she stared, waited patiently
as they secured her seat belt.
She didn't turn
to look at us
staring out the window

but I like to think
I saw the faintest smile
playing in the corner of her mouth
as the car pulled away.

She'll get plenty of bed rest
where she's going
books and telly
free hot meals.
It's probably what she needs.
Come to think of it

it's probably what we all need.

A Letter To An Air Stewardess Found In The Back Of Seat 67A

Dear Waitress Of The Air,
When you are very old, grey, blind and deaf,
disgracing yourself by wetting your tights
each time you sneeze or cough,
then breaking wind when you call out in pain and confusion
when you smell weird (of yeast spread and sick)
please do tell your meals-on-wheels do-gooder
or Help the Aged social worker who is indeed
your only contact with the outside world
that you once refused to lend a poet a pen
on a short flight to Austria
for no reason whatsoever.

Tell them it was back then,
when you were tangerine-coloured
with a ballerina bun, a soft fruit arse,
over-plucked eyebrows and liar eyes.
Tell them how you got quite a little kick
out of the fact you were not even using it,
that biro, right there,
in the tippety tip of the top pocket.
You were keeping it there to look official.
You knew - and we all *knew* that you knew that we knew -
that you had spare ones,

with the airline name written down the side
in the "Luxury Goods" duty-free rip-off trolley.
Yet you forced the poor dear poet to write in lipstick
on the back of a used sick bag.
Didn't you understand that the poet had experienced
a marvellous inspiration upon take off?
It could have been the greatest genius poem
of all of our lifetimes.

Please note that instead of poetry this was what the poet wrote
on that same short flight:

Dearest Sky Barmaid,
with your halloween pumpkin slit for an inane smile
this one is not for you – you sour-faced citrus
but about you – you mottled mandarin-skinned reptile.
I demand you bring me ten more vodkas
as I scrawl these words
blurred and smeared
with carroty sick seeping through.

I hope that you enjoy a miserable monotonous life
like a one-winged bird going in circles
with no real destination or purpose,
your cupreous skin like poor quality leather goods
from all those sunbeds
your jowls sagging from all that hair bun pinning.
Stinking of cheap perfume

your arsehole limp from aeroplane fibre-free foodstuff
and all those rough dry arse-rape searches at every
landing.
I see you baby
I see you with your peach painted talons
clinging to an oxygen mask
whilst you lose that very pen
to an insane suicidal terrorist madman
who uses it to write his demands on your face
mistaking it for an orange Post-it note.
I hope that pen leaks all over your uniform
and dyes your right tit blue.
I also hope you choke on rancid pilot sperm.

Bon voyage!
Seat 66A.

On/Off

We meet on
Oxford Street
it's late
I tell you I hate you
and ask you to leave *my* London
so I can get on with my life
your hair is too long and scruffy
and I tell you
then I kiss you
and you say
stop kissing me please Salena
and then we kiss again
we sit on a bench
share a roll-up
and make talking noise
then we kiss
up close
in a doorway
grinding against a wall
until you say
you have to go.
No! I say
No, actually, I have to go
and I jump on
some random passing bus

stopping at a red light
leaving you
gawping there
unshaven
with bad hair
you are nothing without me
I take the wrong bus home
and into my bed alone
I am so glad
we sorted absolutely
nothing
out.

I'm Gonna Move To Hastings

I'm gonna move to Hastings
pick up where I left off
I'm gonna get drunk every day
with drunks who piss me off.
I'm gonna move to Hastings
become the fancy blow-job queen
get a job in a dirty dark pub
with a broken ice machine.

I'm gonna move to Hastings
where it's two quid for triple house gin
I'll go mental, crazy-eyed
wear no shoes and go through bins.
I'm gonna move to Hastings
sleep with bouncers and not the bands
in the toilets I'll have fishermen finger me
with tattooed, corn-rough hands.

I'm gonna move to Hastings
spend my benefits on the booze
get off with people's boyfriends
get in catfights which I'll lose.
I'm gonna move to Hastings
smoke cheap fags and score shit gear
get bloated on chips and vodka
have weird sex beneath the pier.

I'm gonna move to Hastings
teenage mothers pissing on the street
white stilletos without irony
blistering on their feet.
I'm gonna move to Hastings
where it's as cheap as chips
and the bad boys, they crack on
even when the condom rips.

I'm gonna move to Hastings
go as low as high can go
we all suck on Hastings rock
it's the hardest rock I know.
I'm gonna move to Hastings
bed-sit with a vague view of the sea
sign on the sick, save my medication
burn these poems, when they burn me.